A Troll too Far
and other scary stories

Written by
Caroline Repchuk and Geoff Cowan

Illustrated by
Robin Edmonds, Chris Forsey and
Claire Mumford

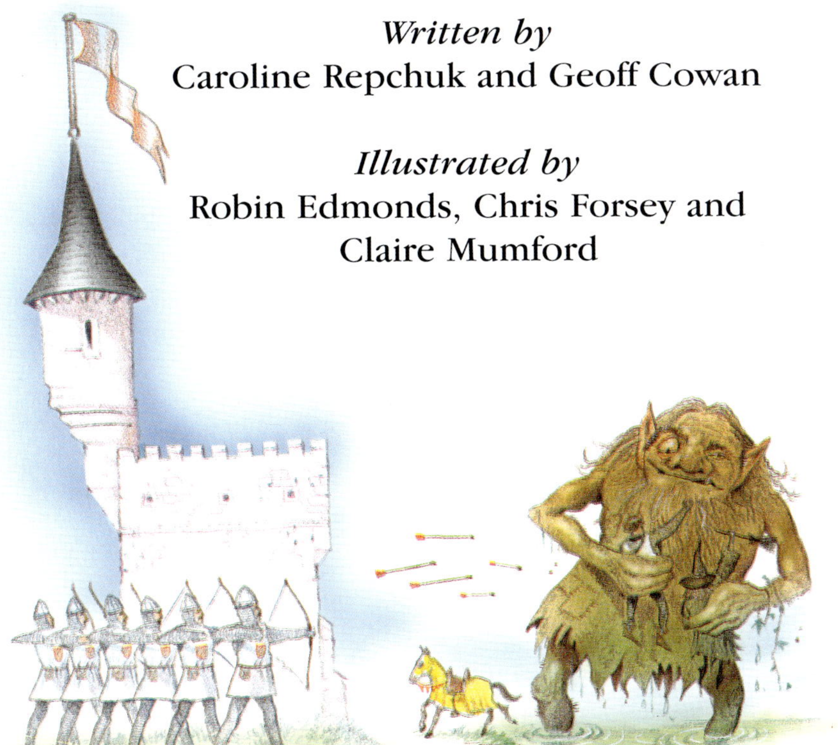

This is a Parragon book
First published in 2000

Parragon
Queen Street House
4 Queen Street
Bath BA1 1HE, UK

Produced by
The Templar Company plc,
Pippbrook Mill, London Road,
Dorking, Surrey RH4 1JE UK

Edited by Caroline Repchuk

Designed by Caroline Reeves

This material has previously been published in *Spooky Stories*,
published 1999

Printed and bound in Spain
ISBN 0 75253 406 8

Contents

A Troll too Far

Once upon a time, in a faraway fairytale kingdom, there lived a king with a problem — a very big, very nasty problem indeed. Now, the king lived in a proper fairytale castle, with towers and turrets, ballrooms and battlements, a wide, deep moat and a drawbridge. And underneath that drawbridge lived and lurked a very large, very smelly, very HUNGRY troll!

The king was in despair. Could no one save them from their castle prison? Then, just as he had almost given up hope, a lumbering shape came looming through the mist.

"*I* will rid you of this terrible troll," boomed a deep and dreadful voice. As the mist cleared the king saw to his horror that the voice belonged to an even larger, even uglier, even smellier troll! But what could the king do? He was certainly not about to argue!

And so the new troll leapt into the moat and a fearsome fight took place. The two trolls thrashed and splashed, bit and scratched, pulled and tugged, roared and gnashed their teeth. They sent tidal waves crashing around the moat, and shook the castle to its foundations!

Finally, after three days and nights of monstrous struggling, the old troll was forced to accept defeat, and he stomped away into the distance, cursing and shaking his fist.

And so it was that one day the king called for the captain of his army. He told him to instruct his archers to fire arrows from the castle, with a royal decree attached. These arrows landed close to the nearby village, where the villagers soon found and read the message. The village buzzed with the news that the king was offering to grant anything within his power to whoever could rid him of the terrible troll.

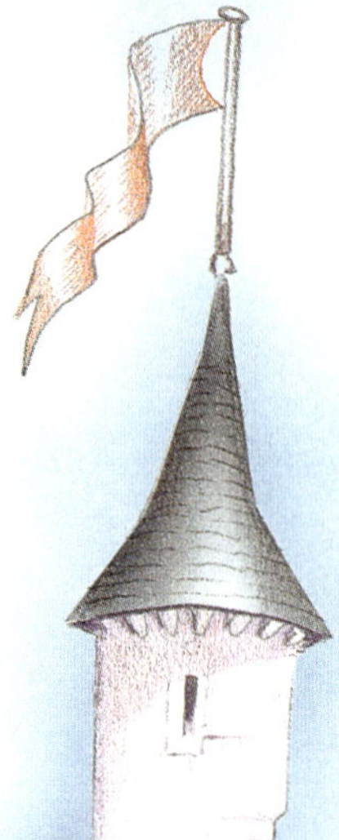

From the village, the news spread throughout the land, and further still, and soon noblemen, knights and princes were arriving from far and near to take up the challenge, and claim their reward. The greedy troll was delighted. Never had he enjoyed such a feast of fine fare, as he munched his way through each brave (or foolish) challenger.

Now trolls, as you may or may not know, will as a rule eat anything, and this troll was no exception. He guzzled the goldfish that swam in the moat, he snacked on stray sheep that grazed at the water's edge (sheep are incredibly stupid!) and worse still, he stretched out one long slimy arm and snatched anything — or anyone — that ventured across the drawbridge, and gobbled it down in a gulp! Whether jousters or jesters, witches or wenches, paupers or princes, this terrible troll would gorge on them all. And as if all this were not bad enough, this left the poor king and his courtiers with yet another problem — they were trapped in the castle and supplies were getting low, for no-one could cross the drawbridge for fear of being eaten.

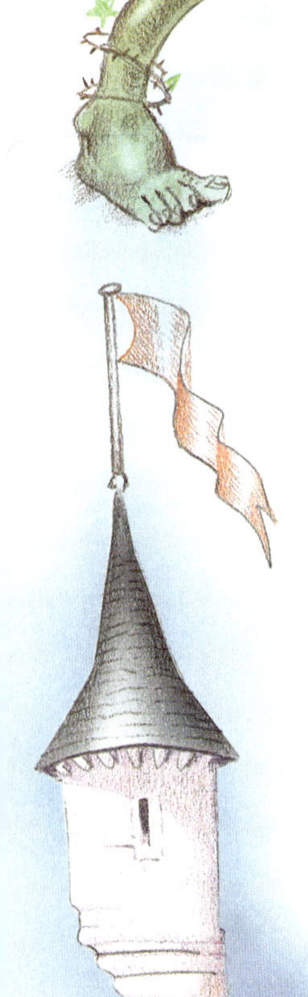

"And now for my reward!" smirked the new troll, with a gleam in his eye, slowly licking his lips. The king shuddered, and clasped the princesses tightly to him. Anything but his precious daughters!

"What is your request," stuttered the king. "I will grant you anything in my power, as I promised."

"I'd like a new home," drawled the troll. "Beneath the drawbridge..."

"Open wide," called young Princess Grace. From beneath the drawbridge, the hideous head of the revolting new troll appeared, mouth open wide to reveal a rotting row of yellow teeth.

"Yum, yum, breakfast!" slobbered the troll. The princess leaned over the drawbridge and poured a vast vat of cakes and cabbages into the troll's quivering, dribbling, open mouth.

For yes, he was huge, he was smelly, he was hideous. But he was also *vegetarian* — and the king was delighted!

Time for a Re-vamp!

I'm a vampire in need of a re-vamp,
Just look at the state of my hair!
I've been searching my wardrobe all morning,
But I can't find a thing I can wear!

I'm a vampire in need of a re-vamp,
With too healthy a glow to my skin,
I've been eating so much I've grown podgy,
When we all know vampires should be thin.

I'm a vampire in need of a re-vamp,
The wrinkles are starting to show,

I know I can't help getting older,
But I really have let myself go!

I'm a vampire in need of a re-vamp,
I've been far too busy of late,
There's been so much to sink my teeth into,
I've let myself slip to this state.

I'm a vampire in need of a re-vamp,
So there's only one thing I can do,
Go on telly and have a makeover,
And soon I'll be back good as new!

A Night in the Haunted House

High up on a lonely hill, surrounded by a great dark forest, stood an ancient, crumbling manor, known as the *Haunted House*. It belonged to a greedy old man, who everyone said was a wizard. He lived in a little cottage in the grounds of the manor, with just his black cat for company. He had no friends to speak of, but he was very happy, because he had a true love. Now, his true love was gold, and he had plenty of it, for he had found a way to make the *Haunted House* serve him well, even though he dare not set one foot inside it himself.

He had pinned a notice to the tall rusting gates of the manor, promising a reward of five hundred gold coins to anyone who could spend a whole night inside it, and charging them five gold coins for the privilege of trying.

Desperate men and brave adventurers came from far and wide, each certain they could withstand the horrors of the *Haunted House*. Some did well, and lasted many hours before fleeing in terror. Back in the safety of the local village inn, they would mutter and gibber and stutter out tales of ghosts so ghoulish, and monsters so terrifying, that their wide-eyed listeners would gasp with horror and congratulate them for staying in the house so long. Others lasted mere minutes before fleeing into the night in shame.

Now one day, there came a man called Titan, whose bravery was legendary. He was known far and wide as the most fearless adventurer, with towering strength and nerves of steel. He paid his five gold coins to the wizard, who rather reluctantly gave him the key to the house. This fellow looked a bit too fearless for the wizard's liking.

That night, Titan stepped through the rusty gates, and strode towards the *Haunted House*. Without hesitating, he unlocked the door and went in. A butler appeared from nowhere, carrying his head under his arm. "Jeeves at your service, sir," he said, creepily. "Follow me."

"Thank you, my good man," said Titan, handing him his coat and following him up the creaking staircase without blinking an eye.

Ancient portraits followed him with their eyes. Titan winked at them as he passed. An empty suit of armour waved. Titan waved back. "Good evening," he said.

Jeeves led him on down a murky passage. A heavy door creaked open and they entered a dark bedroom, with a tattered four-poster bed. Cobwebs hung from the ceiling, and a thick layer of dust covered the furniture. Titan opened the wardrobe and a skeleton came leering out. "Oops, sorry to disturb you," Titan said, brushing the cobwebs from a chair.

The startled butler looked at Titan in amazement. Was this man scared of anything?. "Tea, sir?" Jeeves asked. "Herman will bring it up right away."

Moments later Herman, a dribbling two-headed ogre, appeared with Titan's tea. "Thank you," said Titan, pouring the tea without flinching. "That will be all."

And so it went on through the night. The inhabitants of the *Haunted House* did their worst. Ghouls wailed and werewolves howled. Mummies rose up from their tombs and staggered through the room. A ghostly prisoner appeared dragging clanking chains and vanished through the wall. Vampires leered and phantoms jeered.

"This is quite a show!" said Titan, settling back on his pillows, and watching the ghostly goings-on with a cheerful grin.

Meanwhile, down in the little cottage, the wizard kept glancing nervously at the clock, as he shone and polished his precious gold. Slowly the hours passed, and still there was no sign of Titan. Could this be the man who would finally claim the reward?

Back at the house, a fluffy white ghost was hovering over Titan's head, shouting "Boo!" and trying to sound frightening. It was his first night on the job. The startled spooks had had to call out all reserves — how were they going to frighten this man of steel?

Titan reached up and grabbed the ghost in one mighty swoop. "Just what I need. You'll make an excellent extra pillow," and he stuffed the little ghost behind his head, lay back and was soon snoring soundly. Hour after hour the exasperated spooks kept up their grim hauntings, but Titan just carried on sleeping, oblivious to their efforts.

Then, as the village clock chimed four o'clock faraway in the distance, Titan began to stir. He twitched and wriggled and shook his head, then turned over, pulling the pillows tighter to him. But still he was not comfortable. He tossed and he turned, groaning and grumbling, but it was no good.

There was something lumpy underneath his pillow that was keeping him from settling back to sleep. He opened his eyes. The exhausted ghouls surged forward, renewing their efforts to terrify him.

"Oh, are you chaps still up?!" said Titan, surprised. "Don't you have beds to go to?" The weary ghosts shook their heads in exasperation. Titan felt about under his pillow. What was it that was lodged under there, keeping him awake? Just then, his hand wrapped around something small and soft and furry. He felt a shiver run down his spine. Slowly he pulled out his hand from under the pillow and there, trembling in fright was a tiny little white mouse. Titan let out an almighty scream! He leapt from the bed and raced for the door.

Down he fled through dusty passages and darkened stairways, then disappeared, still screaming and hollering, into the night.

Through his window, the wizard cackled in delight as he watched him fleeing. He hugged his bag of gold to him, and rubbed his hands together with glee.

"I knew he'd crack," he chuckled. "Something gets to all of them in the end!"

The Toast Ghost

A hungry ghost wished for some toast,
"I'd eat a loaf!" he'd often boast.
The words he longed someone to utter,
Were "Here's some toast with lots of butter!"

The ghost lived in a ruined house.
He shared it with a little mouse.
It squeaked, "No toast! Don't even look!
There is no cooker, nor a cook!"

The ghost despaired, "What shall I do?"
The mouse replied, "If I were you,
I'd seek a cafe or a restaurant,
Ask them to make the toast you want!"

The ghost soon found the perfect spot.
He dreamed of toast, lovely and hot.
He waited for the cafe to close,
While smells all toasty teased his nose.

He went inside and found the kitchen.
For buttered toast the ghost was itchin'!
Then something white behind the door,
Floated softly to the floor.

The nervous ghost took off in fright –
He found he'd lost his appetite.
"That's really put me off my tea!"
But let me tell, 'tween you and me –
It was the chef's white hat he saw.
That ghost, he don't eat toast no more!

Freaky Friends

Having an old witch as her next-door-neighbour was the last thing that Victoria Vampire wanted. No sooner had Winnie moved in, complete with her broomstick, cauldron, pointed hat and all manner of pots and potions, than weird things began to happen.

Whenever Winnie stirred up a magical brew indoors, a mass of stars and sparks would fly out of the chimney of her tumbledown old cottage like a fantastic firework show.

They whizzed safely beyond her own little cottage garden — and landed in the grounds of Victoria's dark and spooky house instead! Victoria's clean washing was soon spotted with sooty marks and two big holes were burned in her best black cloak.

Then there was the smell, or more precisely, the stinky pong! Whatever was bubbling away in Winnie's cauldron, it was definitely *not* leek and potato soup. The awful aroma wafted across into the dark turrets of Victoria's home. In no time it had disturbed Victoria's precious colony of bats that lived in the attic. They poured like black treacle out of a small skylight and fluttered away to hide in a dark, distant cave. And as if losing her pets wasn't bad enough, Victoria had to keep every door and window tightly closed against the stink. It was enough to make her flash her fangs in anger!

But there was worse to come. Winnie's two cats, Scratch and Sniff, were mouse-mad, they chased them non-stop. So one day, when they spotted some by Victoria's woodshed, the mean-eyed cats set off in hot pursuit. The trouble was that Victoria had just entered the shed to fetch some logs for her fire. Now, being a vampire, she didn't like going out in daylight and, as usual, was wearing her dark sunglasses. So she didn't see Scratch and Sniff slink into the shed — she just felt the sting of their claws as she tripped over them and they lashed out at her legs. Victoria let out a blood-curdling scream, the startled cats screeched 'YEOWWL!', wood went flying and so did Victoria! She crashed into the door, bumping her head and breaking an arm off her precious sunglasses.

Meanwhile, the cats sulkily slipped away, having lost the mice who had taken advantage of all the commotion and disappeared.

Victoria tried to balance her broken sunglasses back on her nose. Then she felt inside her mouth and winced — she had broken one of her fine fangs when she fell over. That was the last straw!

"That does it!" she hissed. "I'm going to have a not-so-neighbourly word with that pesky witch!"

Victoria marched straight out of her own gate, up the front path to Winnie's cottage and thumped on the door. But Winnie was in the back garden, practising some spelling. She was concentrating so hard that she did not hear the visiting vampire. Winnie waved her wand at a carpet-beater lying on the lawn. Nearby, a large, dusty rug hung on the washing line.

"Eye of newt and lizard's spleen, carpet-beater start to *clean!"* she chanted.

"There you are!" cried Victoria, stomping around the side of the cottage. "I've got a bone to pick with you."

"Oh, good. Come inside, then. I'm hungry, too," said Winnie, smiling innocently at her.

Victoria was about to set Winnie straight and give her a piece of her mind, when she suddenly stopped dead in her tracks. Something was floating towards her.

It was the carpet-beater. Instead of giving the rug a good dusting, it swished and swiped at Victoria.

"Ooh! Aagh! Help!" she wailed as the carpet beater chased her out of Winnie's garden and all the way home. There she sat and sulked until the moon rose.

"Enough's enough!" she thought. "It's time I taught that tiresome witch a lesson!" She stomped out into the darkness, and was soon hard at work in Winnie's garden, pulling up all the magic plants and trampling on the special herb patch. Then she spied Scratch and Sniff curled up fast asleep in a basket by an open window. Reaching in with both hands she caught hold of their long whiskers and pulled with all her might — Ping! Ping! Ping! The furious cats howled in pain and leapt in the air. But, using some special

vampire magic of her own, Victoria turned herself into a bat and took off into the night. But she hadn't flown far when, suddenly, something whizzed past her like a rocket. It was Winnie on her broomstick.

Caught in its slipstream, Victoria was tossed about like a leaf in a storm. She had just made a bumpy landing on Winnie's lawn when the witch swooped down and landed right on top of her! As Scratch prepared to pounce, thinking bat might make a tasty alternative to mouse, Victoria changed back with a flash. But she was bruised and breathless.

"Ohh! My back!" Victoria groaned.

"Deary me!" wailed the witch. "It's all my fault! I had no idea it was you! Here, please let me help!"

Victoria was too weary to argue. And help Winnie certainly did.

Over the next few days, nothing was too much trouble for her. She insisted that Victoria rest at home in bed while she cooked a surprisingly tasty beetroot soup. It was such a deliciously deep red colour that Victoria had to have some.

"It would have been better if those pesky cats hadn't dug up my herbs, mind you," said Winnie. While Victoria guiltily enjoyed another bowlful, Winnie searched her spell book

"Aha! I knew it was here somewhere!" she said. Winnie waved her wand and chanted something about taking care of canines. Then, in a flash, Victoria's two beautiful, long sharp teeth were perfect again.

"*Fangs* very much," she joked.

Further spells repaired the holes in Victoria's cloak, cleaned up her washing, and brought her bats back to the loft. Another spell made Winnie's broom sweep up the wood-shed. Scratch and Sniff eagerly caught every mouse in Victoria's house (which made up a bit for losing their whiskers!). Victoria felt ashamed for trying to teach the kind witch a lesson.

"I feel so much better," smiled Victoria, getting up at last. "You're a wonder, Winnie!"

"Nonsense! Nothing like a *spell* in bed," the witch replied, modestly, as she gave her new-found friend a hug.

Lonely Hearts

Fun-loving troll, dirty and smelly,
With damp slimy skin and big hairy belly,
Nice muddy fingers and grubby wet toes,
Hot, steamy breath and rings through each nose.

With stains on his shirt and holes in his socks,
Teeth that need cleaning and knots in his locks,
Tears in his trousers and scuffs on his shoe,
He's waiting to meet someone lovely like you.

He likes dirty ditches and hiding in holes,
Is certain to win when he fights other trolls.
Is very attentive, will woo you with roses,
After he's used them to pick both his noses.

He lives on his own, in a dark stinking pit,
Oozing with slime and covered in spit.
Now feeling lonely, he hopes there's a chance
He can meet someone similar for fun and romance!